creepy creatures

CONTENTS

Published by Creative Education
P.O. Box 227, Mankato, Minnesota 56002
Creative Education is an imprint of
The Creative Company
www.thecreativecompany.us

Design and production by Ellen Huber
Art direction by Rita Marshall
Printed in the United States of America

Photographs by 123rf (Adrian Hillman), Bigstock
(South12th), CanStock (cosmln, defun), Dreamstime
(Cameramannz, Chrisp543, Isselee, Eric Krouse,
Cosmin Manci, Mhchuang, Rasmus Christian Fejer
Nielsen), Getty Images (Gail Shumway), iStockphoto
(Antagain, Evgeniy Ayupov, Chang Ching Hwong,
Eric Isselée, Александр Ковальчук, SteveStone,
TommyIX), Science Photo Library (Patrick Landmann),
Shutterstock (alslutsky, Robert Biedermann, Evok20,
kurt_G, Pigdevil Photo, Jose Ignacio Soto, Arno
van Dulmen), SuperStock (NaturePL), Veer (defun,
Leaper, pzAxe)

Library of Congress Cataloging-in-Publication Data
Bodden, Valerie.
Beetles / by Valerie Bodden.
p. cm. — (Creepy creatures)
Summary: A basic introduction to beetles,
examining where they live, how they grow, what
they eat, and the unique traits that help to define
them, such as their ability to make sounds or glow.
Includes bibliographical references and index.
ISBN 978-1-60818-231-2
1. Beetles—Juvenile literature. I. Title.
QL576.2.B63 2013
595.76—dc23   2011050278

CPSIA: 040913 PO1675
9 8 7 6 5 4 3 2

beetles

VALERIE BODDEN

CREATIVE EDUCATION

You are playing
outside on a warm day.
Suddenly, something
small and colorful
lands near your feet.
You look down.

It is a beetle!

The dogbane beetle is named for the kind of plant it likes to eat

Beetles are insects. They have three body parts and six legs. Beetles have two **antennae** (*an-TEH-nee*). Most beetles have two pairs of wings. The front wings are thick and hard. They cover the thin back wings. The back wings are used for flying.

A beetle's front wings spread apart when it flies

Many beetles are black.

But some are red, green,

blue, orange, or gold.

Some beetles are so small

that you can see them

only by using a **microscope**.

But other beetles are as

big as a grown-up's hand!

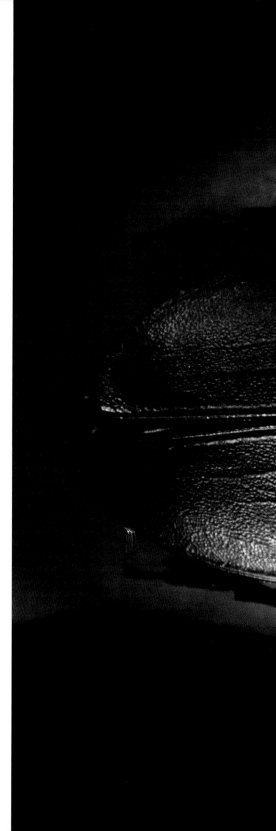

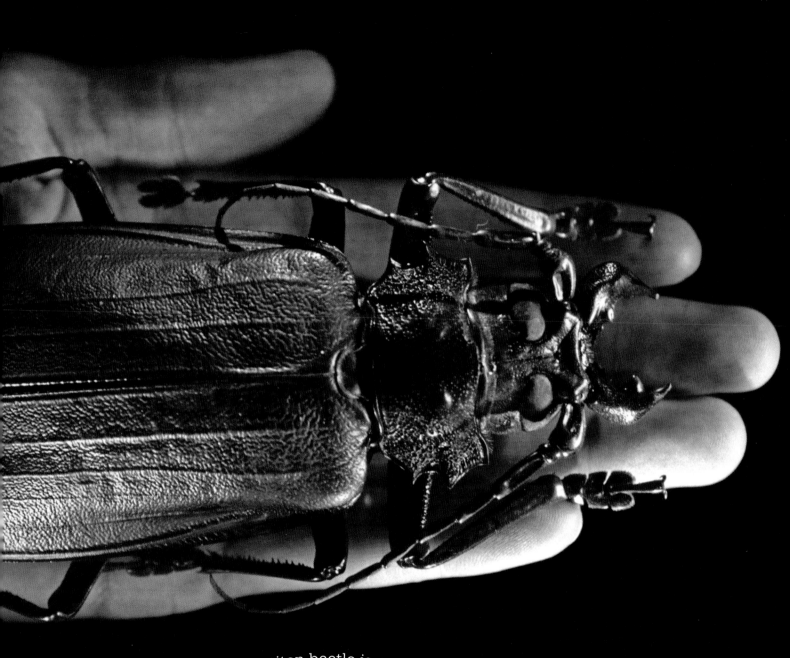

The titan beetle is one of the biggest insects in the world

About 5,000 kinds of ladybug live in the world today

This Hercules beetle is shown at actual size

There are more than 350,000 kinds of beetles!

Ladybugs are common beetles in many places.

Rhinoceros beetles are some of the biggest beetles.

Great diving beetles live in fresh water and eat tiny fish

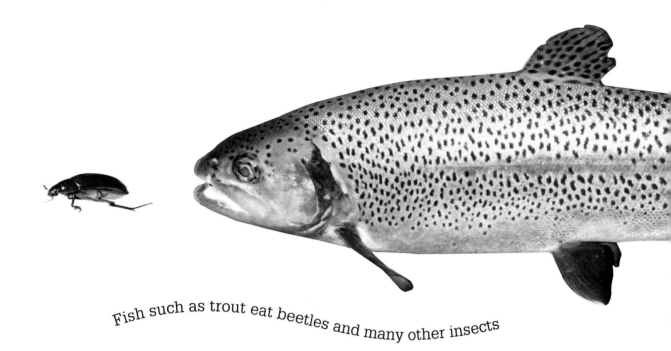

Fish such as trout eat beetles and many other insects

Beetles live almost everywhere on Earth. But they do not live in the coldest places or in oceans. Many beetles live underground or in trees. Others live in lakes or ponds. Beetles have to watch out for **predators**. Birds, frogs, fish, and bats all eat beetles.

A Colorado potato beetle larva eats the leaves of potato plants

Female beetles lay eggs.
A **larva** comes out of each egg. The larva looks like a small worm. The larva eats and grows. Then it molts, or loses its skin and grows a new one. After a while, the larva grows into a **pupa**. The pupa changes into an adult beetle. Some beetles live only a few months. Others can live more than 10 years!

These are larvae of the cockchafer (left) and stag beetle (right)

Dung beetles that roll dung into balls are called "rollers"

Some beetles eat plants. Others hunt
for caterpillars, snails, and even small
frogs. Some beetles eat rotting logs,
dead animals, or dung (animal waste).

Some beetles, such
as fireflies, can glow.
They use their lights
to send messages
to other beetles.
Some beetles can
make sounds. Click
beetles make a loud
clicking noise.

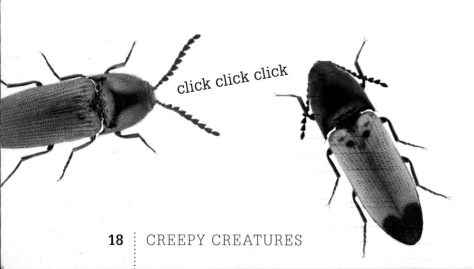

click click click

A firefly lights up to get another firefly to come to it

Long ago, people in Egypt thought dung beetles were **sacred**. People in many parts of the world think beetles are good luck. Some people even keep beetles as pets. It can be fun finding and watching these winged creepy creatures!

The scarab (left) was a sacred beetle to Egyptians

MAKE A LADYBUG

Make your own ladybug by painting a paper plate black.
Paint another plate red with black spots. When the paint
dries, cut the red plate in half. Hold the tops of the two
halves together, and spread the bottoms apart to make
an upside-down V shape for wings. Fix the wings to the
black plate with a brass fastener. Glue a half-circle of
black paper above the fastener for a head, then add some
wiggly eyes!

GLOSSARY

antennae: feelers on the heads of some insects that are used to touch, smell, and taste things

larva: the form some insects and animals take when they hatch from eggs, before changing into their adult form

microscope: a machine that makes something look much bigger than it really is

predators: animals that kill and eat other animals

pupa: an insect that is changing from a larva into an adult, usually while inside a covering or case to keep it safe

sacred: describing something that people worship or praise

READ MORE

Helget, Nicole. *Beetles*. Mankato, Minn.: Creative Education, 2008.

Sexton, Colleen A. *Beetles*. Minneapolis: Bellwether Media, 2007.

WEB SITES

Enchanted Learning: Beetle Printouts

http://www.enchantedlearning.com/subjects/insects/beetles/printouts.shtml

Learn about different kinds of beetles, and find beetle coloring pictures.

National Geographic Kids Creature Features: Dung Beetles

http://kids.nationalgeographic.com/kids/animals/creaturefeature/dung-beetle/

Check out videos, pictures, and facts about the dung beetle.